# BAPTIST HISTORY

WRITTEN BY: Tom Nettles

ILLUSTRATED BY: Robert Nettles

Baptist History for Kids



*Illustrator*: Robert Nettles and Valentina Nettles

*Cover Design:* Tessa Avery-Smith

*Editor*: Denise Huffman

*Publisher*: Evan Knies

ISBN 978-1-955295-54-3



*Cover images (from left):* Robert A. Baker, David Benedict, A.H. Newman, Joseph Ivimey, Isaac McCoy

100 Manly Street
Greenville, South Carolina 29601
CourierPublishing.com

PRINTED IN THE UNITED STATES OF AMERICA

# DEDICATED TO:

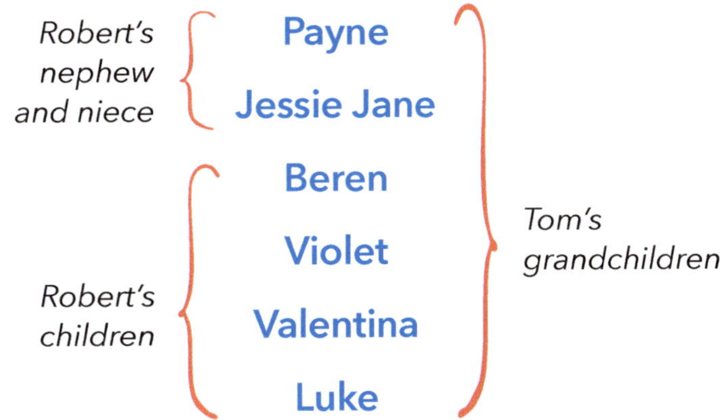


*~ May the gospel bear fruit here and hereafter in their lives ~*

# TABLE OF CONTENTS

# INTRODUCTION

Welcome to a brief story about ***Baptists.*** This is a true story. The people are real and really did the things described here. History is a long story from the creation of the world all the way to the present. No human can know all of history; only God knows that. None can know all the reasons that make things happen. Only God knows that. Ephesians 1:11 teaches, among other things, that God "works all things according to the counsel of His will." The Bible, though, is the Word of God and has a lot of history in it. The history it gives us is to show how things got to be the way they are. It doesn't say everything but enough to give us needed perspective.

So it is with this story about the Baptists. It is history and will give briefly some of the stories about how the people called "Baptists" came to be. It will have names. These are real people, not fictional characters that this writer invented. This history will give a short discussion of how Baptists began in the modern world and came to be a large Christian denomination. It will explain some beliefs. These are some of the "doctrines" that define Baptists. It will describe how what Baptists believe determines what they do. Sometimes difficulties have developed in Baptist life. These have often caused controversies. This history will try to explain some of those. Hundreds – no, thousands and millions – of people have made Baptists what they are today. This history will mention several names that have been influential in particular areas of Baptist ministry.

As in all histories, this does not tell everything. I have tried to make it accurate in what it does tell. I hope it will inspire you to do more reading in Baptist history, Baptist doctrine, and Baptist biography.

## WHAT DOES "BAPTIST" MEAN?

The name "Baptist" comes from a word in the Bible. That word means to put a person completely under water and bring him up again. This is called immersion. ***Being baptized is a picture of being dead, buried, and rising from the dead.*** That is what Jesus did – He died on the cross, He was buried, and He came back to life and left His grave. When a person is baptized, it means that he believes in his heart that Jesus died to forgive his sins and rose from His grave to give him eternal life.

***When should a person be baptized?*** Jesus commanded His disciples to baptize people who also became disciples of Jesus (Matthew 28:19). When a person hears the gospel and believes it, he should be baptized. Only those who hear and believe the gospel should be baptized. Because Baptists did not sprinkle babies, but baptized only those who could hear and believe the message, their enemies called them "Baptizers" or "Baptists."

There are many examples of baptizing believers in the Bible. Jesus was not a sinner; He was the Savior. By His death, burial, and resurrection, Jesus would save sinners from eternal punishment. He was baptized by John the Baptist to show that He would die and rise again. Every person who believes that Jesus did this should follow Jesus's example (Romans 6:3–5). The apostle Paul did this when he became a Christian. A man named Ananias was sent to Paul. Paul had hated Christians and had imprisoned them and sometimes joined in killing them. He was baptized because he had come to believe in Jesus (Acts 9:17, 18). The people who were saved through the preaching of the apostles were baptized (Acts 10:47, 48; Acts 16:15, 33; 18:8). A man from Ethiopia was reading the Bible from the book of Isaiah. A follower of Jesus, Philip, found him and told him that the Bible verses he was reading were about Jesus. He told this man from Ethiopia about Jesus dying for sinners and being raised from the dead. The Ethiopian believed and then Philip baptized him (Acts 8:37, 38).

*Philip baptizing the Ethiopian eunuch.*

***Baptists practice baptism as it was done in the New Testament.*** They gave a picture of death, burial, and resurrection. They baptize only those who believe that message. They do not, therefore, baptize babies. That is why they are called Baptists.

## HOW DID BAPTISTS BEGIN?

A Christian movement known as the Reformation began over four hundred years ago. Many years after the times of the New Testament, churches began to do things for salvation that were not taught in the New Testament. After many years of such wrong teaching, some preachers and teachers began to reject these unbiblical practices. They began to teach that only the Bible should be followed in what the church believes and does. ***This focus on the Bible, on Jesus alone as qualified to save sinners, and on faith as the only way to receive Jesus's saving work was called the Protestant Reformation.*** This started in the year 1517. Martin Luther, a Catholic monk, disagreed with some Catholic teachings not found in the Bible. He wanted to discuss these with other teachers. He wrote about the teachings he wanted to discuss in a paper called "The Ninety-five Theses." This paper led to the discussion of many other teachings and to a separation of many churches from the Roman Catholic church. Some of its other leaders were John Calvin, Martin Bucer, and Ulrich Zwingli. In England, John Wyclif, William Tyndale, and Thomas Cranmer were important leaders.

When the Reformation became strong in England, kings and queens soon declared that every English person must become Protestant. They established the Anglican Church, or Church of England. Their confession of faith was called the "Thirty-nine Articles." Their form of worship was prescribed by the *Book of Common Prayer*. They did not stop baptizing all babies but stated in their confession "the baptism of young children is in any wise to be retained in the church." Many of the people believed that baptism accomplished forgiveness of sins, since the confession said: "They that received baptism rightly are grafted into the Church; the promises of the forgiveness of sin, and our adoption to be the sons of God by the Holy Ghost, are visibly signed and sealed." By law, all had to be a part of the established Anglican Church.

As the Reformation grew in England, many preachers wanted the church members to show that they were sincere followers of Jesus. They wanted worship based on the Bible, not that demanded by the *Book of Common Prayer*. These were Puritans. They wanted to give the Lord's Supper only to those who clearly lived to honor Jesus. Some came to believe that so strongly that they separated from the Church of England to form more pure congregations. ***These were Separatists.*** Some of these congregations were persecuted and left England to go to Holland.

While in Holland, some of the Separatists began to teach that infant baptism was the cause of corrupt churches. They came to believe from studying the Bible that only true believers should be baptized and be members of the church. They were influenced by a church group in Holland known as "Anabaptists," or re-baptizers. One of the first Englishmen who taught this was John Smyth. He did not believe everything that the Anabaptists believed, so in 1609 he baptized himself and then baptized his entire congregation as believers. His confession of faith said, "Baptism is the external sign of the remission of sins, of dying and of being made alive, and therefore does not belong to infants." When he decided that he should not have baptized himself, he wanted to join the Anabaptists.

*John Smyth baptizing himself. (VN)*

A church member named Thomas Helwys disagreed with Smyth's decision to join the Anabaptists, called Mennonites. He came back to England and started the first Baptist church in England. Helwys wrote a book about the errors of all the churches that still baptized infants, *The Mystery of Iniquity.* In this book, he also told the king that he had no right to make all his people be a part of the Church of England. Helwys said that the king is only a man, is not in the position of God and has no authority over the souls of the people. Thomas Helwys was put in prison and died there in 1616. This group of Baptists grew and were known as ***General Baptists.*** They were courageous and were willing to suffer for their faith.

Another group of Baptists, known as ***Particular Baptists,*** started a church in 1638. John Spilsbery was the first pastor. Particular Baptists wrote confessions of faith in 1644 and 1677. In 1689, a year after the "Act of Toleration" had been made, close to one hundred Particular Baptist pastors made a public declaration of this confession and signed it. They differed from General Baptists in the way they understood certain doctrines about God's sovereignty in salvation. Spilsbery's personal confession said that God did "elect and choose some certain number" of sinful persons for "eternal life in his Son." He taught that this shows the purity and power of God's grace and justice.

In America, a man named Roger Williams (1603–1684) said that the government should not interfere in church doctrine or worship. As you can see, he died before the "Act of Toleration" was passed. Also, he said that persons must be allowed to worship according to their own conscience. He was forced to leave Massachusetts Bay because of these beliefs. With the help of the Indians, he founded the colony of Rhode Island. Soon after arriving there, Williams became convinced that only people who could hear and understand the gospel and then truly believed it should be baptized. He started the first Baptist church in America in Providence, Rhode Island, in 1638. He wrote a book about liberty of conscience entitled *The Bloody Tenent of Persecution for Cause of Conscience.*

A man named John Clarke (1609–1676) came to believe the same thing and started a Baptist church in Newport, Rhode Island, just a short time later in 1638. He was persecuted by Massachusetts authorities also. Obadiah Holmes, Clarke's friend, was whipped severely for being a Baptist. Holmes said that God supported him during this brutal whipping. Holmes testified that God gave him strength to endure the whipping. He told those who whipped him, "You have struck me as with roses." John Clarke told that story in a book entitled *Ille News from New England.*

*Obadiah Holmes whipped for being a Baptist.*

Thomas Gould also was persecuted for doubting infant baptism. After much harassment, he began a Baptist church near Boston in 1665. From Boston, William Screven (1629–1713) went to Maine and started a Baptist church in 1682. This church moved to Charleston, South Carolina, and became the first Baptist church in the South.

Elias Keach (1667–1701) and several other gospel preachers started Baptist churches in Pennsylvania. Keach was nineteen when he came to the New World from England.

He was not a Christian. His father, Benjamin Keach, was a famous Baptist preacher in London. Elias had memorized some of his father's sermons. When he came to America, he began to preach them. As he preached one of these sermons, he was converted. He was baptized and then began a Baptist church near Philadelphia. These churches soon started the first Baptist association in America, the Philadelphia Association (1707). The churches in that association believed like the Particular Baptists in England.

During the First Great Awakening in the 1700s, Baptists became more numerous. New Baptist churches were started in New England, with Isaac Backus (1724–1806) as a leading preacher. He also was a strong voice for separation of church and state and liberty of conscience. Baptists grew and evangelized many destitute areas through their work in the Philadelphia Association. John Gano (1724–1804) was an active evangelist sent out by the association. Baptists grew rapidly during this time. The Separate Baptists led by Shubal Stearns (1706–1771) and Daniel Marshall in the South spread Baptist life into Georgia, Virginia, North Carolina, and Kentucky. Within fifty years after the Awakening, there were almost four times as many Baptist churches as before the Awakening.

*Isaac Backus*

## WHAT DO BAPTISTS BELIEVE?

Baptists have been eager to show the world and other Christians what they believe. Among the many ways they have done this has been in writings known as "Confessions of Faith." The church has written and used these kinds of documents since the time of the New Testament (see 1 Timothy 3:16). General Baptists and Particular Baptists have written important confessions of faith. Also, Baptists in America have written such documents. Among the most important are the New Hampshire Confession (1833), the Abstract of Principles (1859), and the Baptist Faith and Message (1925, 1963, and 2000).

Baptist confessions of faith include a statement that the Bible is the only true authority for what a Christian believes. To its words and doctrines, "nothing at any time is to be added." Writers of the Bible knew that God inspired what they wrote (2 Timothy 3:16). Because God inspired the Bible, Baptists believe that all of it is true. The confession of faith, therefore, is a statement of what a group of people believe that the Bible says. They join with each other because they share that belief. Important areas of belief are presented in each Baptist confession.

*First, Baptists put many things in these confessions believed by all Christian groups.* They believe in the Trinity, that God is in three persons: Father, Son, and Holy Spirit. They believe with all Christians that God created the entire universe. He created Adam and Eve and that all persons in the world have come from them. Baptists believe that Jesus is the Son of God who came to earth by being born of the virgin Mary. He lived life as a man while still being God, dying for sinners as a man, and rising again. He went back to heaven, has sent His followers to preach the gospel, and will come again.

*Second, Baptists also believe many of the things that other Protestants believe.* They believe that all persons are sinners without strength or desire to help themselves. They believe that we are made right with God and forgiven of sins only because of what Jesus did in our place. His perfect obedience is given to those who trust Him. They believe that God gives us this salvation by His mercy and grace. They believe also that God causes His people to do good works. He does this through the power of the Holy Spirit. They believe that at death true believers go immediately to heaven. Those who have not trusted Christ go immediately to hell.

*Third, Baptists differ from most other Christian groups, however, by their conviction that only true Christians should be baptized and become members of the church.* This conviction is called "regenerate church membership." They believe churches should have pastors (or elders) and deacons to help the members learn and serve. They believe that these churches should worship together on every Lord's Day and seek to help other people believe the gospel.

## WHAT DO BAPTISTS DO?

***Baptists worship together.*** The Bible says that each church should have a pastor qualified to preach. Christians should listen to sermons together to be taught right thinking and right acting from the Bible. They should pray following biblical patterns for prayer both in private and in public worship. For some encouragement and instruction from the Bible, read Matthew 6:5–15, Luke 18:9–14, Ephesians 1:15–21, and 2 Thessalonians 2:16–17. Also, Baptists sing in their worship services to encourage and instruct one another as Ephesians 5:19, 20 and Colossians 3:16 exhort. This shows that they depend on God and that they worship God. Baptist churches practice baptism in view of the congregation. In this way, new believers show their faith in the saving power of the death, burial, and resurrection of Jesus. Church members should take the Lord's Supper together frequently because Christ commanded it. This reminds the church members of the grace of Christ in dying for us.

***Baptists join together to help preachers receive an education.*** This education focuses on learning how to interpret the Bible. This often involves learning to read both Greek and Hebrew. Also, these preachers are taught the doctrines of the Bible. This includes studying systematic theology and historical theology. It also is important to study the history of doctrine as well as the history of the church. There are even classes that concentrate on the Bible's teaching about how to minister to the personal and spiritual needs of the people in the church. A very effective school in England for this purpose was Bristol Baptist Academy, which began in 1720. Bernard Foskett was its first teacher. He also served as pastor of Broadmead Baptist Church. Another effective school to train ministers of the gospel was the Pastors' College founded by Charles Spurgeon. It began with one student in 1856 and trained hundreds of students to preach the gospel. In the United States, Baptist colleges provided for the study of Bible and doctrine. When The Southern Baptist Theological Seminary in 1859 in Greenville, South Carolina, was founded, many began to study at seminary. The seminary was devoted specifically to training men for pastoral ministry. It now is in Louisville, Kentucky, and has trained thousands of preachers and other church workers. James Petigru Boyce wrote about theological education and had the most influence in founding the school.

*Baptists write books and publish newspapers.* Baptists write books about the Bible, doctrine, Christian living, being a Christian family, biographies, and history. These books can help Christians to be mature in what they believe. Among the thousands of books written by Baptists, a very important one in the twentieth century was entitled *Why I Preach the Bible is Literally True,* by W.A. Criswell. Such books can help Christians to be witnesses for the gospel. Baptists also publish newspapers. These provide meaningful information about churches, what missionaries are doing, and other ministries and activities Baptists promote. Among the

The Baptist Courier

OWNED AND CONTROLLED BY THE BAPTISTS OF SOUTH CAROLINA

Vol. 60 Greenville, S. C., August 16, 1928 No. 33

papers are The Baptist Record in Mississippi, The Christian Index in Georgia, and The Baptist Courier of South Carolina.

***Baptists send missionaries to places where the gospel is hardly known, or perhaps not known at all.*** William Carey (1761–1834) had a powerful influence in making Baptists a missionary people. He wrote a book entitled *An Enquiry Into the Obligations of Christians to Use Means for the Conversion of the Heathens*. He then went to India where he stayed as a missionary from 1791 until his death in 1834. He translated the Bible into around thirty languages spoken by different groups in India. Adoniram (1788–1850) and Ann Judson (d. 1826) were the first Baptist missionaries from America. They were sent by another Christian denomination in 1812 and became Baptists after they got to India. Their influence, along with that of Luther Rice, caused Baptists in America to begin a nationwide missionary organization called "The General Missionary Convention."

AN
ENQUIRY
INTO THE
OBLIGATIONS OF CHRISTIANS,
TO USE MEANS FOR THE
CONVERSION
OF THE
HEATHENS.
IN WHICH THE
RELIGIOUS STATE OF THE DIFFERENT NATIONS OF THE WORLD, THE SUCCESS OF FORMER UNDERTAKINGS, AND THE PRACTICABILITY OF FURTHER UNDERTAKINGS, ARE CONSIDERED,
BY WILLIAM CAREY.

For there is no Difference between the Jew and the Greek; for the same Lord over all, is rich unto all that call upon him. For whosoever shall call on the name of the Lord shall be saved. How then shall they call on him, in whom they have not believed? and how shall they believe in him of whom they have not heard? and how shall they hear without a Preacher? and how shall they preach except they be sent?

PAUL.

LEICESTER:
Printed and sold by ANN IRELAND, and the other Booksellers in *Leicester*; J. JOHNSON, St. Paul's Church yard; T. KNOTT, Lombard Street; R. DILLY, in the Poultry, *London*; and SMITH, at *Sheffield*.
[Price One Shilling and Six-pence.]
MDCCXCII.

*William Carey's book that inspired missionaries.*

Lottie Moon (1840–1912) was a Southern Baptist missionary. She went to China in 1873 and worked faithfully starting schools for children, making evangelistic trips to different places, and helping women understand the gospel. She died on Christmas Eve. She had made Southern Baptists more aware of missions. The "Lottie Moon Christmas Offering" is named in her memory. William and Anne Bagby went as a missionary couple to Brazil in 1880. Through godly zeal and wisdom and in spite of serious opposition, they established a thriving Baptist work in Brazil. On one occasion, William, while preaching, was knocked unconscious by a rock thrown at him by a protester. When he regained consciousness, he stood up and began preaching again. Six of the nine Bagby children also became missionaries.

*William Bagby knocked unconscious by a rock thrown by a protester. (VN)*

# BAPTISTS AND CONTROVERSY

Christian faith often includes defending the truth of the Bible. Sometimes this creates controversy. The world is sinful and tries to avoid Christian truth. Even in the church, false teachers might try to change the Bible's message. God's direct instruction to Adam was the first target of Satan's attack – "Has God indeed said?" (Genesis 3:1). The apostle John warned against the "spirit of error" in the church (1 John 4:6). Christians are told to contend for the faith that has been given to us by God (Jude 3). Paul warned that "some will depart from the faith" (1 Timothy 4:1). Peter also warned, "There will be false teachers among you" (2 Peter 2:1).

Some early teachers in the church denied that Jesus was really a true man. They were called Gnostics because they believed they had a special knowledge that was not in the Bible. That is certainly the "spirit of error." Many faithful teachers showed from the Bible that Jesus was a true man, that He was born, that He suffered, that He died, and that He rose from the dead. Even during the life of the apostle John, this was happening. That is why he wrote, "Every spirit that confesses that Jesus Christ has come in the flesh is of God, and every spirit that does not confess Jesus," that is, that He has come in true human flesh, "is not from God" (1 John 4:2–3, ESV).

Others would say that Jesus was not truly God. They were called Arians because they believed the teaching of a man named Arius. He said that Jesus, as the Son of God, was created and, therefore, not truly God. This was a terrible error. Again, faithful teachers showed the Bible's teaching that Jesus was God and that He Himself was Creator. Paul presented this truth strongly in Colossians 1:15–20. A famous Christian statement known as the Nicene Creed said Jesus was "begotten, not created, of the substance of the Father, of one substance with the Father." That kind of language was important to affirm that Jesus was indeed true eternal God.

Some taught that because Jesus was both God and man, then He must be two persons. True teachers in the church had to declare very firmly that Jesus was just one person. Nestorius taught the error, and Cyril, a pastor in Alexandria, Egypt, opposed that teaching as heresy.

A man named Pelagius denied original sin and the necessity of special grace to save sinners. He taught that Adam's sin affected only him. Each person is born in the condition Adam was in when he was created. Humans are not born with sinful natures, Pelagius taught. He believed that people could live righteously. They would be accepted by God because of their righteousness. He went on to say that God's grace of salvation is given according to our merits. A devoted pastor named Augustine pointed to Romans 5, 1 Corinthians 15, and many other Scripture passages to correct Pelagius's error. He showed, like Ephesians 2:3 says, we are "by nature children of wrath." He also showed the meaning of Paul's statement, "By grace you have been saved through faith, and that not of yourselves; it is the gift of God, not of works" (Ephesians 2:8–9).

***Trinity* means *"three in one."*** In Christian doctrine, it means that God is one God but eternally exists in three persons. Other religions deny this idea. Some persons claiming to be Christians, such as the Unitarians, have also denied it. From the New Testament times all the way to today, Christians have seen the importance of this doctrine. Every generation has to defend it because it is biblical truth and important for salvation. Paul prayed for the church at Corinth, "The grace of the Lord Jesus Christ, and the love of God [the Father], and the communion of the Holy Spirit be with you all" (2 Corinthians 13:14).

Creation is another important Christian doctrine that has been resisted and even rejected. God's creation of the world, including Adam and Eve, is rejected by evolutionists. Creation, however, is taught throughout the Bible. It is important to believe it for a right view of God and His purpose for the world. God told Israel through Isaiah, "Have you not known? Have you not heard? The everlasting God, the Lord, the Creator of the ends of the earth, neither faints nor is weary. His understanding is unsearchable" (Isaiah 40:28).

All of these doctrines that the church has described and defended are revealed in the Bible and are therefore protected by the church against those who would say, "Has God said?"

Baptists also have seen the need to defend Christian truth. Baptists agree that their main task is to preach the gospel and witness to unsaved people all over the world. If the message preached, however, is not the biblical message, then their preaching is without importance. Any kind of belief that people may put in such a false message also is vain (1 Corinthians 15:14). Disagreement and controversy are often difficult and upsetting. They should be avoided on issues that are unclear or unimportant (Titus 3:9–11). Christian discipleship, however, calls for faithfulness to Christ and His word so we will not be deceived and fall short of the truth (2 Peter 3:17–18).

How have Baptists been involved in this difficult but necessary work? First, the very existence of the Baptist movement depended on the courage and willingness to suffer of those first Baptists. Many of the early Baptists such as John Smyth, Thomas Helwys, John Spilsbery, Hanserd Knollys, John Murton, Benjamin Keach, and Thomas Grantham suffered for their courageous work in teaching their convictions about baptism from Scripture. Their views of baptism helped them see that people should have liberty of conscience. Neither churches nor governments should force people into a religion.

Baptists in America were effective in presenting a biblical case for liberty of conscience. Roger Williams, John Clarke, Isaac Backus, John Leland, Oliver Hart, Richard Furman and others worked to convince people that a nation would prosper and the churches would be purer if liberty of conscience was the law of the land. As a result of their influence, the United States Constitution (Article VI) says, "No religious test shall ever be required as a Qualification to any Office or public Trust under the United States." Also, the first statement in the Bill of Rights (Amendment One) states, "Congress shall make no law respecting an establishment of religion, or prohibiting the free exercise thereof."

Dan Taylor (1738–1813), a General Baptist minister in England in the eighteenth century, discovered that many of the ministers did not accept the doctrine of the Trinity. They also preached and wrote in ways that showed they doubted other important doctrines, including the deity of Jesus. Taylor formed a "New Connection" of General Baptists that insisted on true doctrines. One statement in their confession of faith said, "We believe that our Lord Jesus Christ is God and man, united in one person: or possessed of divine perfection united to human nature, in a way which we pretend not to explain, but think ourselves bound by the word of God firmly to believe."

Andrew Fuller (1754–1815) was an effective preacher, supporter of foreign missions, and theologian. Some people believed that God's sovereignty means that humans don't have responsibility. Fuller presented a strong biblical reason that God's sovereignty does not eliminate human duty. ***Preachers still have a duty to call on sinners to trust in Christ.*** Also, the sinner has a duty to turn from sin and place faith in Christ. Fuller found it necessary to write against several dangerous doctrinal errors. He wrote books seeking to correct the views of Deists who did not believe that God presently was active in the world. They did not believe that Jesus had died for sinners, or that God revealed truth in the Bible. He also wrote against Socinians. They denied that Christ was God in the flesh and preached that the doctrine of the Trinity was absurd. He wrote to correct those who did not believe that repentance

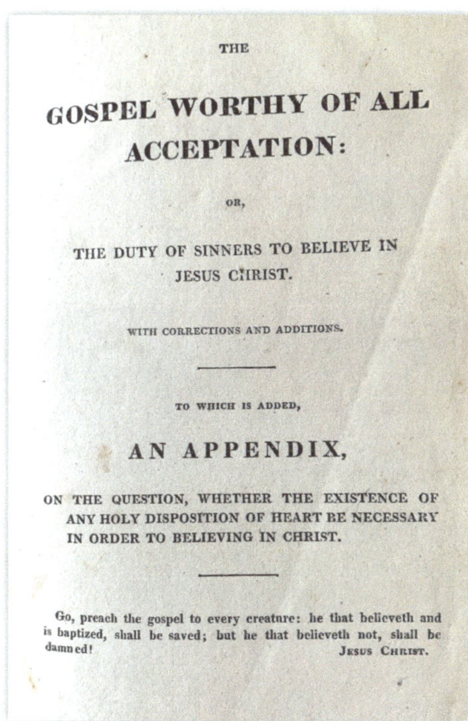

THE

GOSPEL WORTHY OF ALL ACCEPTATION:

OR,

THE DUTY OF SINNERS TO BELIEVE IN JESUS CHRIST.

WITH CORRECTIONS AND ADDITIONS.

TO WHICH IS ADDED,

AN APPENDIX,

ON THE QUESTION, WHETHER THE EXISTENCE OF ANY HOLY DISPOSITION OF HEART BE NECESSARY IN ORDER TO BELIEVING IN CHRIST.

Go, preach the gospel to every creature: he that believeth and is baptized, shall be saved; but he that believeth not, shall be damned!

JESUS CHRIST.

*Fuller on doctrinal errors.*

from sin was a necessary part of saving faith. Fuller wrote a very effective defense of the missionary movement to Parliament when some businessmen who made much money from cheap labor in India wanted Parliament to rule that Baptists must stop their missionary work in India.

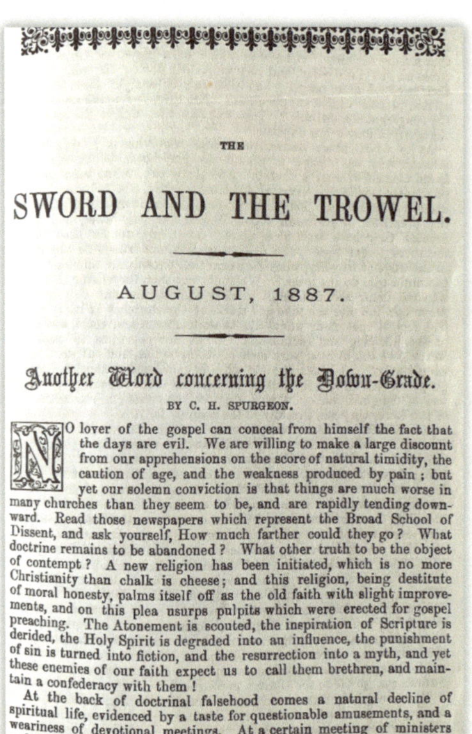

THE

SWORD AND THE TROWEL.

AUGUST, 1887.

Another Word concerning the Down-Grade.

BY C. H. SPURGEON.

NO lover of the gospel can conceal from himself the fact that the days are evil. We are willing to make a large discount from our apprehensions on the score of natural timidity, the caution of age, and the weakness produced by pain; but yet our solemn conviction is that things are much worse in many churches than they seem to be, and are rapidly tending downward. Read those newspapers which represent the Broad School of Dissent, and ask yourself, How much farther could they go? What doctrine remains to be abandoned? What other truth to be the object of contempt? A new religion has been initiated, which is no more Christianity than chalk is cheese; and this religion, being destitute of moral honesty, palms itself off as the old faith with slight improvements, and on this plea usurps pulpits which were erected for gospel preaching. The Atonement is scouted, the inspiration of Scripture is derided, the Holy Spirit is degraded into an influence, the punishment of sin is turned into fiction, and the resurrection into a myth, and yet these enemies of our faith expect us to call them brethren, and maintain a confederacy with them!

At the back of doctrinal falsehood comes a natural decline of spiritual life, evidenced by a taste for questionable amusements, and a weariness of devotional meetings. At a certain meeting of ministers and church-officers, one after another doubted the value of prayer-meetings; all confessed that they had a very small attendance, and several acknowledged without the slightest compunction that they had

17 29

*Spurgeon's "Down-grade."*

Charles Spurgeon opposed the liberal trend in theology that developed in the nineteenth century (1888–1892) among Baptists in England. He called this the "Down-grade." Several vitally important doctrines were being questioned. Some popular preachers doubted the full inspiration of the Bible. Several rejected the deity of Jesus. Like Pelagius centuries ago, some did not believe that the whole human race was included in Adam's sin and often thought that the entire story of Adam's disobedience was a mere fable. Most pastors teaching these errors would not teach that Jesus Christ died as a substitute for sinners. Some taught that the Holy Spirit was not truly a divine person. Piling many errors together, some of the "modern thinkers" would not proclaim that justification before God was based on the righteousness of Christ. Spurgeon was ridiculed in the newspapers, censored by the Baptist Union, and lost friendships because of his courageous writing and preaching. He separated from the Baptist Union in 1888.

In America, a controversy among Baptists beginning around 1833 brought a split between Baptists in the North and Baptists in the South. They disagreed about several things concerning the operation of their missions, publishing, and educational organizations. A major problem that gave intensity to these disagreements was the position of each section, North and South, on slavery. Because many Baptists in the South owned slaves and defended their right to do so, they began to be excluded from participation in the missionary organizations. Baptists in the North believed this was a serious moral issue. Baptists in the South started a new convention to support missions in 1845, called the Southern Baptist Convention. After the Civil War, some attempts to reunite the Baptist conventions failed.

In the 1850s, a controversy developed about Baptist history. The disputed question was, "Where did Baptists come from?" This was called the "Landmark Controversy." Some Baptists taught strongly that Baptists did not come from the Reformation but had always existed since New Testament times. An early leader of this group was J.R. Graves. Others believed that present day Baptists came from the English Reformation. This controversy was not really theological, for both groups believed that Baptist churches were true New Testament churches. Even today, Baptist writers and Baptist churches disagree on this question.

An early controversy among Southern Baptists about Scripture happened at The Southern Baptist Theological Seminary in 1879 over the teaching of C.H. Toy. He accepted a kind of biblical study called historical criticism. This kind of study had to deny the inerrancy of Scripture. John A. Broadus,

Basil Manly Jr., and J.P. Boyce, though they were friends with Toy, opposed his viewpoint. Toy resigned from teaching in the seminary.

American Baptists also had controversies over a developing theological trend called "Modernism," or "Liberalism." This movement was led by such thinkers as William Newton Clarke, Cornelius Wolfkin, Shailer Mathews, Walter Rauschenbusch, and Harry Emerson Fosdick. In general, they denied all the basic historic convictions of the Christian faith because they did not think that those doctrines stood the test of modern thinking. They said they wanted to follow God in the same way that Jesus followed God and loved His neighbor. They did not believe the full truthfulness and beneficial character of the entire biblical text. They did not accept the Trinity, the deity of Christ, the sinful depravity of humanity, the substitutionary death of Christ, the reality of hell, or the priority of evangelism as the church's mission. Many separations occurred among the Northern Baptists over these severe disagreements.

In addition to the controversy over C.H. Toy, Southern Baptists had controversy in the 1920s over the teaching of evolution at Baptist schools. In 1926, the Southern Baptist Convention adopted this statement: "This Convention accepts Genesis as teaching that man was the special creation of God, and rejects every theory, evolution, or other, which teaches that man originated in, or came by way of, a lower animal ancestry." Though this clear stance was taken against evolution, prohibiting its teaching was not entirely successful.

Also, controversies over the Bible continued to develop. In the late 1950s, a book called *The Message of Genesis* denied that several events recorded in the book of Genesis actually happened. The writer of the book, Ralph Elliott, was dismissed. In the early 1970s, a Bible commentary set, *The Broadman Commentary*, led to another controversy over this same issue. Was Genesis a true record of events? Also the question concerning the inspiration of Scripture caused real concern. One of the editors of the commentary, Clifton Allen, denied that the Bible was verbally inspired. It could not therefore, be without error.

These controversies eventually developed into a long, hard, convention-wide controversy over the true character of the biblical text. This was called the "Conservative Resurgence," which started in 1979. Southern Baptists reclaimed their historical commitment to the full truthfulness of the Bible. As a result, many pastors and Baptist churches that did not receive that view left the Convention and started new church organizations. Among other doctrines, the Conservative Resurgence affirmed that the Bible contains no error in its teaching. It also was clear on the Bible's teaching on the Trinity, sinful humanity's need for salvation, and that His salvation comes only by faith in Jesus Christ because of His dying for us and rising from the dead to assure us of eternal life.

These conflicts are not pleasant and often divide friends. Participants in controversy must make sure that their willingness to engage in potential disagreement, and even separation, is not over minor issues, or issues on which there is not a clear biblical position to defend.

# WHO ARE SOME BAPTISTS YOU SHOULD KNOW ABOUT?

John Bunyan

**John Bunyan** (1628-1688) was a Baptist preacher in Bedford, England. Before he was converted to Christ, he was a tinker – he repaired pots and pans. Bunyan was known in the town of Bedford for his profane language. He related the events concerning his conversion in a book entitled *Grace Abounding to the Chief of Sinners*. The government put him in prison in 1660 for preaching the gospel as a Baptist. He was there for twelve years and while in prison wrote a wonderful book entitled *Pilgrim's Progress*. Every child should know this story. He became well known as a preacher. One of the most educated men in England said he would trade away all of his learning to be able to preach like the tinker.

John Bunyan in prison. (VN)

*William Kiffin*

**William Kiffin** (1616–1701), when he was nine, lost both his parents in a terrible disease that killed many people in London. He was converted to Christ under the influence of Puritan preaching. He also learned much about the Christian life through hearing them preach. He became a Baptist when he listened to John Spilsbery preach. He then started a Baptist church in London around 1640 and served as its pastor for sixty-one years. He became rich through selling wool and once gave King Charles II 10,000 pounds in English money. He used his substantial wealth to relieve the poor. Also, he paid fines for his fellow Baptists to keep them out of prison and sometimes from being put to death. One son of Kiffin was poisoned by a Catholic priest in Venice. The son had been bold in pointing out the errors of Catholicism. Two grandsons were sentenced to death in1685 for their attempts at defending the liberties of Protestants in England. One of them, Benjamin Hewling, said, "I am not ashamed of the cause for which I lay down my life; and as I have engaged in it, and fought for it, so now I am going to seal it with my blood." He wanted all his relatives to know "how precious an interest in Christ is when we come to die." William Kiffin told what a great comfort it was to him to "observe what testimony they left behind of the blessed interest they had in the Lord Jesus, and their humble and holy confidence of their eternal happiness." Kiffin helped write both the First and the Second London Confessions of faith for Particular Baptists. In a controversy with John Bunyan, he wrote a book explaining that only baptized believers should participate in taking the Lord's Supper in a Baptist church.

**Benjamin Keach** (1640–1704) was a tailor who became a pastor in England. He began preaching as a General Baptist but changed to Particular Baptist. Keach endured persecution and his church was harassed because of certain religious laws in England. Keach said that persecution would refine and purify Christians and make them grow in faith and patience. He wrote books for children to help them learn how to spell and read and also about Christianity. He wrote books for adults and other pastors to teach them how to interpret the Bible. For example, the Bible compares the Holy Spirit to fire. Among many, one suggestion made by Keach was this: "Fire gives light, so the Holy Spirit gives light, or illuminates the understanding." Keach also was the first pastor to introduce the singing of hymns as a regular part of congregational worship. This was very controversial in his church. He also wrote long poems such as "War With the Devil" and "The Heavenly Lover." His church became one of the most important and effective Baptist churches in London.

*Benjamin Keach*

John Gill

**John Gill** (1697-1771) began in 1720 to serve in London as pastor in a place called Southwark. This is the same church Benjamin Keach had started. He served there until his death in 1771. Gill wrote strong defenses of the Christian faith in answer to the objections of unbelievers. He also explained Baptist beliefs when other writers misrepresented them or sought to prove them wrong. This pastor wrote a commentary on the entire Bible – every verse. After that he wrote an excellent systematic theology called *Body of Divinity*. When people aware of his study habits wanted to emphasize the certainty of a thing, they would use the phrase, "As surely as Dr. Gill is in his study." Critical observers think that Dr. Gill did not emphasize evangelism in the way that he should. His sermons, however, show a clear presentation of the necessity of and nature of repentance and faith. They are clear that only Jesus Christ can save sinners.

**Andrew Fuller** (1754–1815) was a Baptist pastor. He was a friend of William Carey. He served as pastor in Kettering, England, from 1782–1815. He wrote an important book entitled *The Gospel Worthy of All Acceptation.* This book influenced Baptists to begin their work in foreign missions. Mr. Fuller also wrote important works defending the truth of Christian doctrine and also about the necessity of God's grace in salvation. In his personal confession of faith, Fuller wrote, "I firmly and joyfully believe that the kingdom of Christ will yet be gloriously extended, by the pouring out of God's Spirit on the ministry of the word." Fuller worked and prayed in light of that conviction. It drove him to serve as the leader of the "Particular Baptist Missionary Society" from 1792 until his death in 1815.

*Andrew Fuller*

*Charles Spurgeon*

**Charles Spurgeon** (1834–1892), born the same year that William Carey died, is known by many Christian people as the "Prince of Preachers." He served as pastor in London at the Metropolitan Tabernacle for thirty-eight years. Over 3,000 of his sermons were published. Also, he wrote many other helpful books such as *Around the Wicket Gate* to help people have true faith in Jesus as Savior.

Spurgeon, near the end of his life, took a courageous stand against some very poor theology developing in the Baptist Union of England. During the first month of this controversy, called the "Down-grade Controversy," Spurgeon preached on "The Infallibility of Scripture." Infallibility means that the Bible cannot teach any error. Spurgeon said, "This book is inspired as no other book is inspired, and it is time that all Christians avowed this conviction. Where are we if our Bibles are gone? Where are we if we are taught to distrust them? If we are left in doubt as to which part is inspired and which is not, we are as badly off as if we had no Bible at all."

George Liele

**George Liele** (1750–1820), converted as a slave in 1772, became active in evangelistic work. His witness led to the conversion of several other slaves. His converts helped establish the first two Black Baptist churches in the South, called "Colored Churches" in the records of that time. David George, converted around 1773, was one of the original members when the Silver Bluff Church was constituted in Silver Bluff, Georgia, and served as its pastor. Liele was set free by his master to have an itinerant ministry that led to the formation of worshipping cells of slaves on several plantations and smaller farms. His former owner was killed in the Revolutionary War. The family tried to make him a slave again, but he was able to prove that he had been given his freedom.

Liele went to Jamaica in 1782 with his wife and four children. He planted the gospel ten years before Carey went to India. He also did mission work in Nova Scotia and Sierra Leone, where he established the first Baptist church. He inspired others to become missionary preachers. He wrote the English Baptist John Rippon in 1791, reporting that he had baptized 500 people. Because of his successful work with slaves from Africa, Liele was arrested for sedition. He was thrown into prison. He was later acquitted of these charges. Soon after William Carey went to India, English Baptists began supporting missions in Jamaica as a result of Liele's faithful labors.

*J.P. Boyce*

**J.P. Boyce** (1827–1888) was an influential preacher, editor, and seminary founder among Southern Baptists. His speech, which was printed as a book, entitled *Three Changes in Theological Institutions,* set the pattern for theological education among Southern Baptists. Boyce's ideas about theological education led to the formation of six seminaries among Southern Baptists. He had strong and devoted friends, such as John A. Broadus and Basil Manly Jr., who joined with him in beginning The Southern Baptist Theological Seminary. Boyce taught systematic theology at the seminary. Also, he wrote a textbook of theology entitled *Abstract of Systematic Theology*. He wrote a catechism for children called "A Brief Catechism of Bible Doctrine." The sixth question on the Bible asks, "Ought it, therefore, to be believed and obeyed?" Boyce provided this answer to be memorized: "Yes: as much so as though God had spoken directly to us."

John Jasper

**John Jasper** (1812–1901), born a slave, in Fluvanna County, Virginia, was the last of twenty-four children by his mother, Nina. His father, Philip Jasper, died two months before his birth. Nina is described as sober, elegant, thoughtful, godly, rich in experience, matured in motherliness. John worked on several plantations but lived a riotous life until his conversion in 1839. According to his testimony, he was for six weeks under conviction with his sins piled on him like mountains and his feet sunken into despair. When he cried for mercy, with what he thought might be his last breath, salvation rolled like a flood through his soul. He felt like he could knock the factory roof off with his shouts. His master called Jasper to his office. He listened to his testimony and responded with a handshake saying, "John, I wish you mighty well. Your Saviour is mine, and we are brothers in the Lord."

Jasper began to preach and discovered a natural ability that began to draw crowds of both black and white to hear the slave preacher. He gained his freedom and continued to preach in Richmond, Virginia. His eloquent and picturesque messages of salvation gained a steady stream of converts. He baptized them in the James River. The growing church eventually moved to an old Presbyterian church building. It had to be enlarged twice. This church, the Sixth Mount Zion Church, became the premier place for preaching in all of Richmond. Its membership grew to nearly 2,000. He learned theology from the

Baptist preachers of Virginia. His own study of Scripture strengthened this. He dealt with issues of creation, sin, redemption, heaven, hell, the new birth, the holiness of God, and the glory of Christ in his person and work. One of his most famous sermons was called "The Sun Do Move." It was a defense of the biblical account of a long day in the book of Joshua. His exoneration of God from being the author of sin was entitled "Whar Sin Kum Frum."

W.E. Hatcher, a white Baptist pastor in Richmond, could hardly find enough words to describe the overwhelming positive impact of Jasper. He wrote, "When he became thoroughly impassioned and his face lit with the orator's glory, he seemed to mount above the bondage of words: his feet, his eyes, indeed every feature of his outer being became to him a new language. … You were entranced and borne along on the mountain-side of his passion."

*Sketches of Lottie Moon: Image above is by Robert Nettles, the author's son; image on next page is a replication of Robert's sketch by his daughter, Valentina.*

**Lottie Moon** (1840–1912) – Charlotte Diggs Moon – was born in Albemarle County, Virginia. Her father died when she was thirteen. When she went to Albemarle Female Institute, her teachers said that she was excellent in Latin and French. Her ability to learn languages would help her in China as a missionary. One teacher said, "She writes the best English I have ever been privileged to read." Although she was very smart, she was not an excellent student overall until after she was converted to Christ in 1859. Her conversion came after hearing a sermon by John A. Broadus. She returned to the school and took every course the Institute offered. During the Civil War, she resented the North's invasion of the South. When it was clear that the North would win the war, she said, "We must be just as thankful for sorrows as for joys."

After teaching in Virginia and Georgia, she joined her sister Edmonia in Northern China as a Southern Baptist missionary. In seeing the desperate condition of the Chinese people in their religion, she wrote to Baptists, "We implore you to send us help. Let not these heathen sink down into eternal death without one opportunity to hear that blessed gospel which is to you the source of all joy and comfort."

Her letters home had two elements. One, she wrote frankly of the difficulties of missionary life in China. Two, she issued earnest appeals for the assistance of those who are truly called and prepared for the work. She loved C.H. Toy but broke their relationship because she knew his theological views made it impossible for him to be appointed as a missionary. In 1885, she began Bible teaching and evangelistic work in Pingtu, China. She wrote dozens of letters from there. These letters caused Annie Armstrong to call for a special offering for foreign missions at Christmastime.

Lottie Moon returned home on furlough twice. She went to Japan during the "Boxer Rebellion." She labored for the gospel in China until 1912. That year, she died of starvation on a boat in Kobe Harbor, Japan. She has become a symbol of realistic devotion to the missionary cause among Southern Baptists.

*Parents: This would be a great opportunity to encourage your budding young artists to make their own art projects from some of the pictures in this book!*

*Benajah Harvey Carroll*

**Benajah Harvey Carroll** (1843–1914) was the founder of Southwestern Baptist Theological Seminary. He had been a soldier in the Civil War. Carroll had also served as a pastor for thirty years in Waco, Texas, and taught college for thirty-three years. He came to believe that a seminary in the Southwest was needed. With the support of Baptists in Texas, the seminary began when he was sixty-five years old in 1908. Carroll wrote books about Baptist doctrine and also a commentary on the entire Bible.

Carroll's words to L.R. Scarborough, his successor as president of Southwestern, are memorable. He understood how Baptist institutions must work. "Lee, keep the Seminary lashed to the cross. If heresy ever comes in the teaching, take it to the faculty. If they will not hear you and take prompt action, take it to the trustees of the Seminary. If they will not hear you, take it to the Convention that appoints the Board of Trustees, and if they will not hear you take it to the great common people of our churches. You will not fail to get a hearing then."

*Adrian Rogers*

**Adrian Rogers** (1931–2005), from Florida, began Christian ministry when he was nineteen years old. He graduated from Stetson University and New Orleans Baptist Theological Seminary. He served as pastor of three Baptist churches. The first was in Fellsmere, Florida. Then, from 1964 until 1972, he was the pastor of First Baptist Church of Merritt Island, Florida. From 1972 until 2005, he served the Bellevue Baptist Church in Memphis, Tennessee. While he was pastor, the church grew from 9,000 members to 29,000 members.

Not only was Adrian Rogers a faithful and effective pastor to his own congregation, his preaching and counsel encouraged many others. His broadcasts on radio and television called "Love Worth Finding" were designed to teach non-Christians the gospel and to encourage Christians in consistent spiritual growth. He was particularly influential in the Southern Baptist Convention. He served as president of the Convention on three occasions, being elected in 1979, and again in 1986 and 1987. His influence as a pastor and as president of the Convention greatly aided the theological recovery in the Convention known as the "Conservative Resurgence" already mentioned. The advice that B.H. Carroll gave L.R. Scarborough was exactly what Rogers did. He also served as chair of a committee in 2000 to make a new and clearer presentation of the confession of faith, "The Baptist Faith and Message."

Rogers died soon after he retired in 2005 from his long tenure as pastor.

## WHY IS A KNOWLEDGE OF BAPTIST HISTORY A GOOD THING?

***Studying Baptist history*** helps us see what Baptists have contributed to Christian witness and a safer world. The Baptist emphasis on believer's baptism has helped churches be more evangelistic. Studying history shows how Baptists have been leaders in sending missionaries to other places. Also, a knowledge of Baptist history helps us understand the good results of separation of church and state. Along with that, liberty of conscience has helped society thrive and has caused churches to be clearer in preaching the gospel to lost people.

***Studying Baptist history*** helps one understand the reasons Baptists believe what they believe. When they sought to make clear their broad understanding of the Christian faith, Baptists wrote confessions of faith. Understanding the times and the content of these kinds of statements helps one settle his thinking about Baptist beliefs. Studying history shows how Baptists of the past interpreted the Bible and preached the Bible. ***History shows us a standard of belief.*** Sometimes we are corrected in our personal thinking by knowing about Baptists of the past. On other occasions, history makes it clear that Baptists thought wrongly about an issue and helps us work to correct it.

Connected with that thought is this: ***Studying Baptist history*** helps explain the way in which Baptists are like other Christian groups. Our differences should not make us less thankful for what we share in common. Christians have received in the Bible a revelation from God and knowledge that sin can be forgiven through Christ. When we find that we agree with other Christians on explanations of these truths, we are thankful. The explanations that others give often help Baptists be more devoted and confident in their faith.

*Studying Baptist history* shows the way Baptists are different from other Christian groups. Baptists had to be clear when they stated their reasons for disagreeing with other Christians on some biblical subjects. As one studies history, the reasons for local church independence become clearer. So it is with believer's baptism and teachings connected with that conviction. History gives us a long-term perspective. Sometimes we see clearer in the distance what is blurry up close.

*Studying Baptist history* helps one have a better understanding of the Bible. When we look at Baptist confessions, Baptist agreements with other Christians and Baptist disagreements with other Christians, we also become aware of the Bible's reasons for these things. That probably is the greatest help in studying Baptist history. ***Knowing and loving the Word of God should be a main goal of every Christian's life.*** Seeing the historical importance of studying, believing, and even suffering for biblical truth helps us know it and be determined not to forsake it. As Roger Williams said, "Having bought truth dear, we must not sell it cheap; not the least grain of it for the whole world; no, not for the saving of souls, though our own most precious."

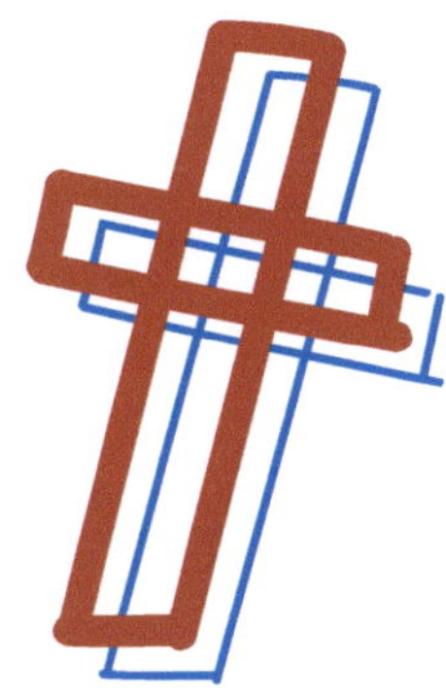

www.ingramcontent.com/pod-product-compliance
Lightning Source LLC
LaVergne TN
LVHW072329100826
845154LV00009B/145

* 9 7 8 1 9 5 5 2 9 5 5 4 3 *